Living in the Rainforest

Patty Whitehouse

Rourke
Publishing LLC
Vero Beach, Florida 32964

www.rourkepublishing.com

PHOTO CREDITS: © Lynn M. Stone: title page, pages: 4, 5, 8, 9, 15, 17, 19, 22; © Devon Stevens: page 10; © Leeman: page 11; © Sirois: page 12; © Dan Wood: page Pg. 14; © Kyle Froese: pages 18; © James H. Carmichael: pages 20; © Long Shots: pages 21.

Editor: Robert Stengard-Olliges

Cover and interior design by Nicola Stratford

Library of Congress Cataloging-in-Publication Data

Whitehouse, Patricia, 1958-
 Living in a rainforest / Patty Whitehouse.
     p. cm. -- (Animal habitats)
 Includes index.
 ISBN 1-60044-186-6 (hard cover)
 ISBN 1-59515-547-3 (soft cover)
 1. Rain forests--Juvenile literature. I. Title. II. Series: Whitehouse, Patricia, 1958- Animal habitats.
 QH86.W482 2007
 578.734--dc22
                              2006017575

Printed in the USA

CG/CG

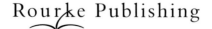

Rourke Publishing

www.rourkepublishing.com – sales@rourkepublishing.com
Post Office Box 3328, Vero Beach, FL 32964

TABLE OF CONTENTS

WHAT IS A RAINFOREST?

Rainforests get a lot of rain. Plants grow well in rainforests. Many kinds of animals live there, too.

Some rainforests are cool. Some rainforests are warm. This book is about warm, **tropical** rainforests.

HOW ARE RAINFOREST PLANTS DIFFERENT?

Many leaves have a point on the end. The point lets rain water drip off the leaf.

Some tree **roots** grow above ground. Other trees are thicker near the ground. Some plants do not have roots at all!

TREES AND VINES

Rainforest trees grow in layers. The tree tops are called the canopy layer.

Woody **vines** grow from the trees. The vines are called lianas. Lianas start near the roots of trees.

HELPFUL AND HARMFUL

We eat many things that grow in the rainforest. **Bananas**, cocoa, and lemons are rainforest plants.

Some plants are not food for animals. Animals are food for the plants! A pitfall trap plant eats ants.

HOW ARE RAINFOREST ANIMALS DIFFERENT?

More animals live in the rainforest than anywhre else. The rainforest is very wet and has tall trees. Many animals can climb and live in trees.

A three-toed sloth can live in a tree for weeks.

IN THE SKY

Morpho butterflies are bright blue. Their wings are as long as your hand.

Many birds fly in the rainforest. Toucans have colorful beaks.

IN TREES AND ON THE GROUND

The poison dart frog lives on the ground. Animals that eat it will get sick.

Howlers are the loudest rainforest monkey. Howler monkeys live in trees.

IN THE RIVERS

Piranhas are fish that live in rivers of the rainforest. They live in **schools**. They use their sharp teeth to eat other fish and other animals.

Caiman hunt in rivers of the rainforest. They are related to alligators.

CAN PEOPLE LIVE IN RAINFORESTS?

People have lived in rainforests for a long time. Many people live in rainforests today.

Some cities were built in rainforests long ago. There are cities in rainforests today.

ENDANGERED RAINFOREST

Rainforests get cut down for wood, paper, or for land. Rainforest animals and plants are **endangered**. Many animals and plants cannot live without the trees.

Glossary

banana (buh NA nuh) — a tropical fruit that is long, curved, and yellow or green

endangered (en DAYN jurd) — in danger of becoming extinct

root (ROOT) — part of a plant that usually grows under the ground

schools (SKOOLZ) — groups of fish

tropical (TROP ik al) — places that are hot and wet

vines (VINEZ) — long stems of a plant

10/06